Happy Reading!

For you loving Grandchildren

— Monica Mahabir

Belandra's Day at the Market

by
Monica Mahabir

ROYARDS PUBLISHING COMPANY

7A Macoya Industrial Estate, Macoya Trinidad W.I.

Telephone: 868-645-0423, 663-6002

Fax: 868-663-3616,659-3515

E-Mail: Royards@aol.com

Website:www.royards.com

written by

Monica Mahabir

First Published: April 2014

Illustrations by: Ian Attong

Printed in China

To my children

Stanley, Megan and Nicole

for their support and encouragement.

and to my grandaughter Isabel Grace Mahabir

Belandra was so excited she could not fall asleep. She stayed awake thinking about her favorite treat. She knew when morning comes she would go to the city market with grandmother Dee.

There is no snow where grandmother Dee lives in this warm tropical island, only bright sunshine and warm rain.

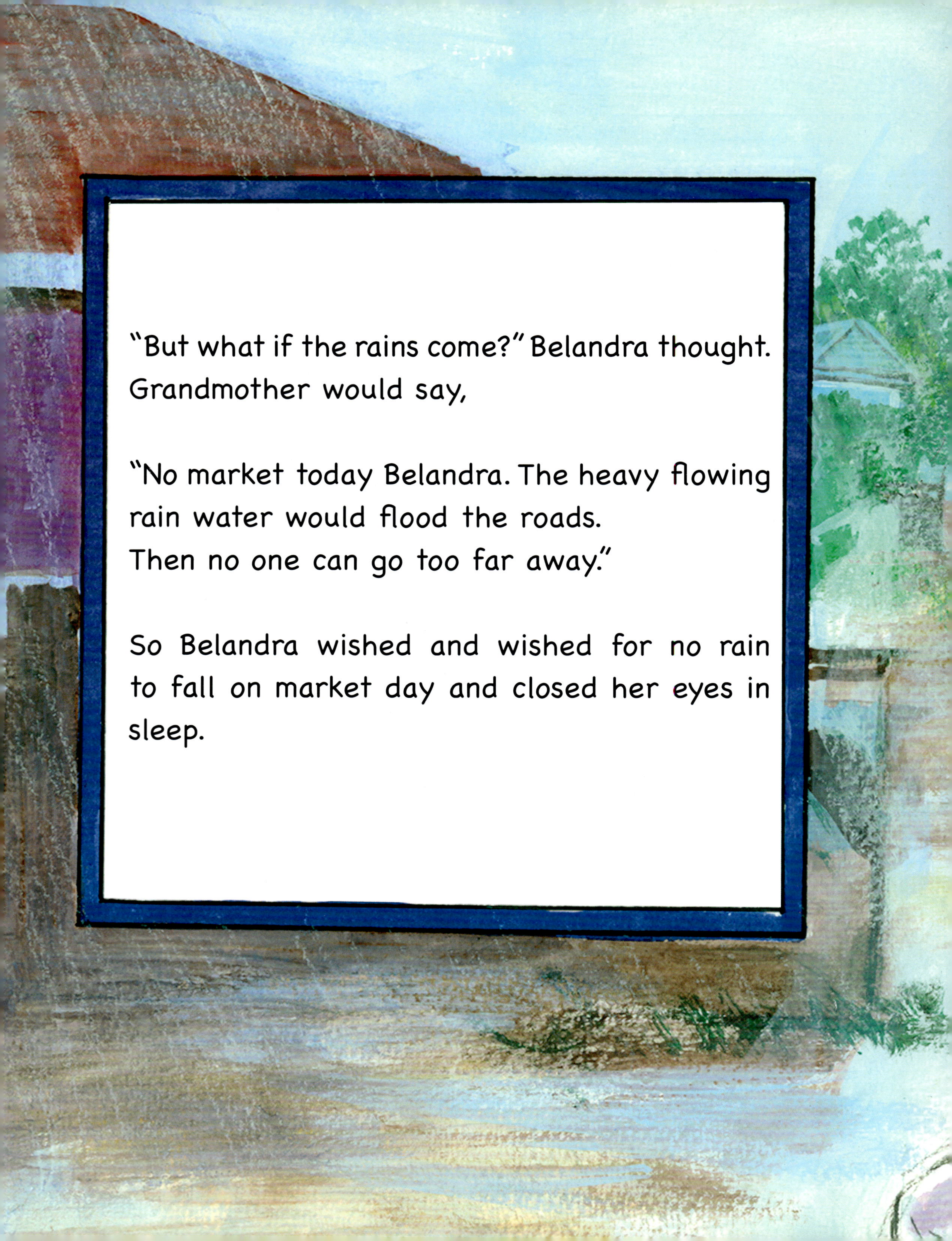

"But what if the rains come?" Belandra thought. Grandmother would say,

"No market today Belandra. The heavy flowing rain water would flood the roads. Then no one can go too far away."

So Belandra wished and wished for no rain to fall on market day and closed her eyes in sleep.

Belandra dreamt the morning sun rising above her, blazing into a bright sunny day. She heard the hum of the rapid wing-beats of hummingbirds. She saw butterflies unfolding golden wings on marigolds and bees sipping nectar from flower to flower.

The wind carried the scent of sweet market fruits. The sounds on the streets began to come alive! Vans honked aloud teet-teeet, rushing people off the streets.

Vendors yelling "sweets, sweets, sweets. Now it's time to buy some treats!"

Belandra's mouth dribbled as she saw rows and rows of sugar cakes, rice cakes, fudge and coconut bakes.

The next morning Belandra woke up to sunshine, as the rooster crowed his morning song.

" No rain today, my wish has come true!" Belandra exclaimed.

"Today is my special day. Grandmother would buy me my favorite treat at the market."

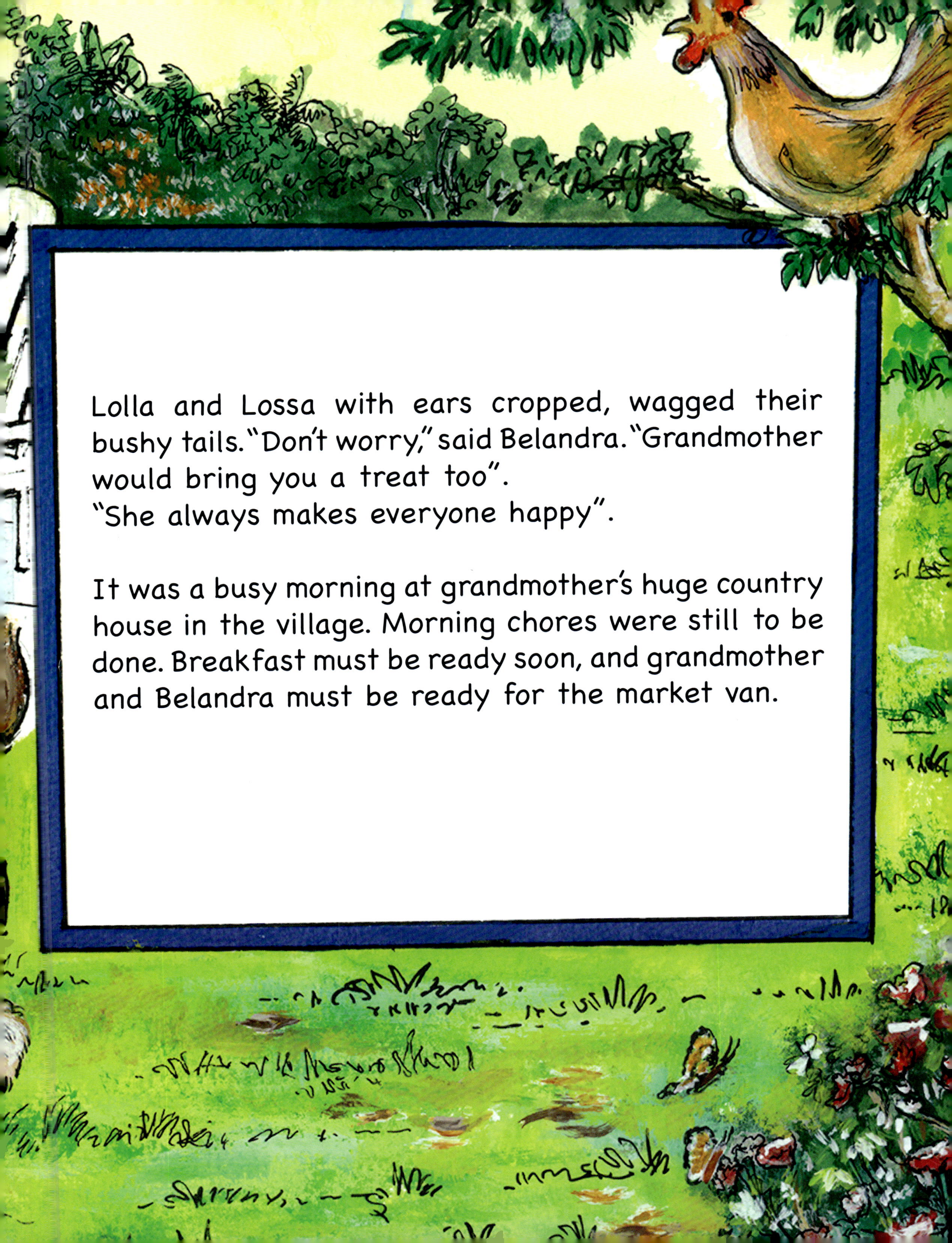

Lolla and Lossa with ears cropped, wagged their bushy tails. "Don't worry," said Belandra. "Grandmother would bring you a treat too".
"She always makes everyone happy".

It was a busy morning at grandmother's huge country house in the village. Morning chores were still to be done. Breakfast must be ready soon, and grandmother and Belandra must be ready for the market van.

Belandra swept the kitchen floor. She dusted the breakfast table carefully gathering bits and pieces of wayward crumbs. She would feed them to the hungry chicks before the sun goes down.

Belandra remembered to fold the paper napkins just as grandmother did.

She shaped them into small triangles with flowers on the front.

"Now I must place one for each person in the family", she said. Belandra thought she would never be finished placing napkins since so many relatives ate at grandmother's huge country house every weekend.

"But I must now hurry", Belandra decided. She quickly placed the last folded napkin, then sat down close to her eight year old cousin to chat about holiday fun together.

Belandra knew very soon that uncles, aunts, cousins and unexpected guests would come to feast on grandmother's hot cakes and guava jam .The smell of fried plantains, and freshly baked coconut buns drew everyone to the breakfast table.

They ate and ate, chatted and laughed, for so much fun there was.

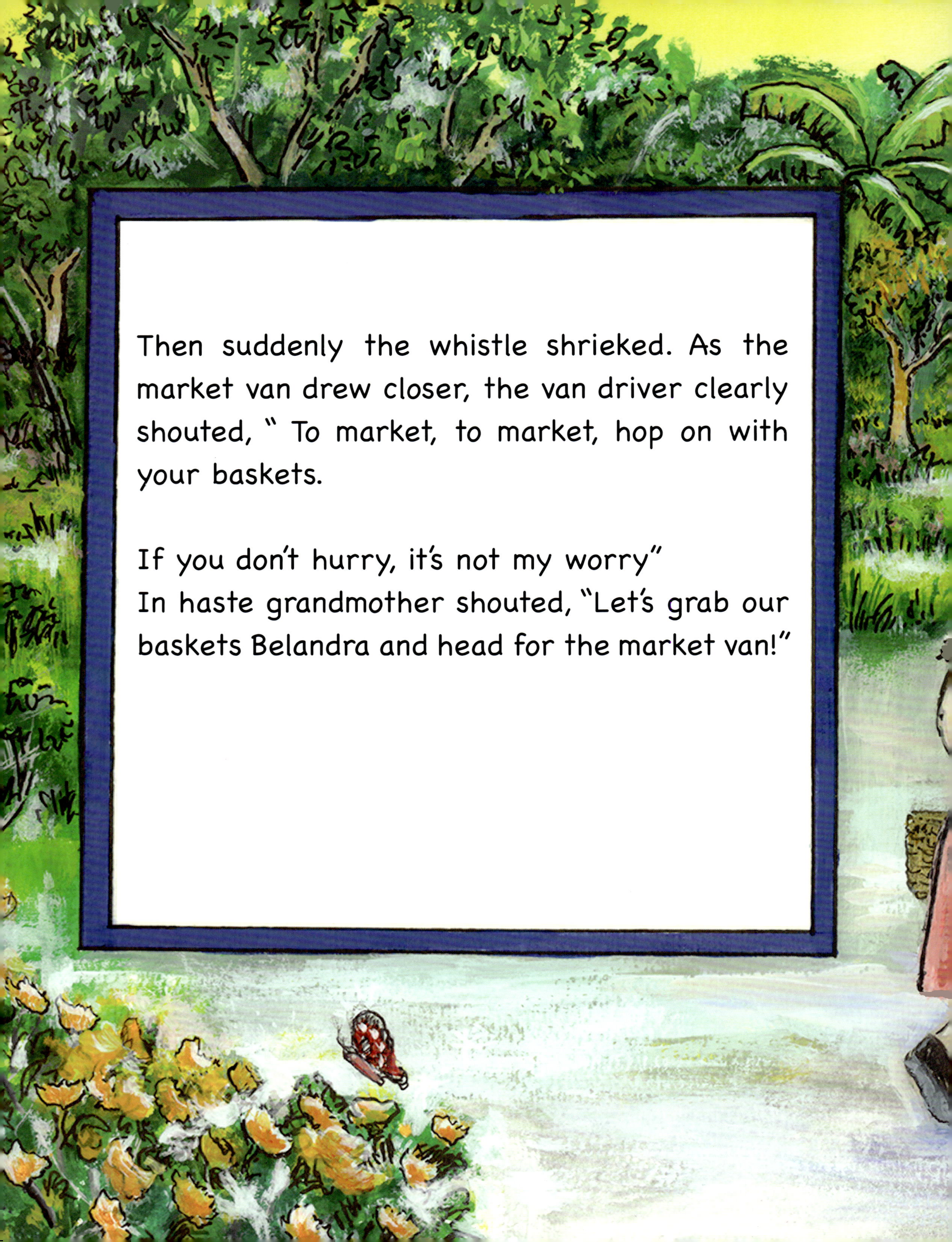

Then suddenly the whistle shrieked. As the market van drew closer, the van driver clearly shouted, " To market, to market, hop on with your baskets.

If you don't hurry, it's not my worry"
In haste grandmother shouted, "Let's grab our baskets Belandra and head for the market van!"

The cool morning breeze rushed through the window where Belandra sat.

As the wind brushed over her cheeks, she drifted into a quiet moment.

Belandra began thinking about her treat. She imagined licking her lips to trap the juice from running wildly , all over her chin. Then suddenly the whistle shrieked. The market van came to a stop.

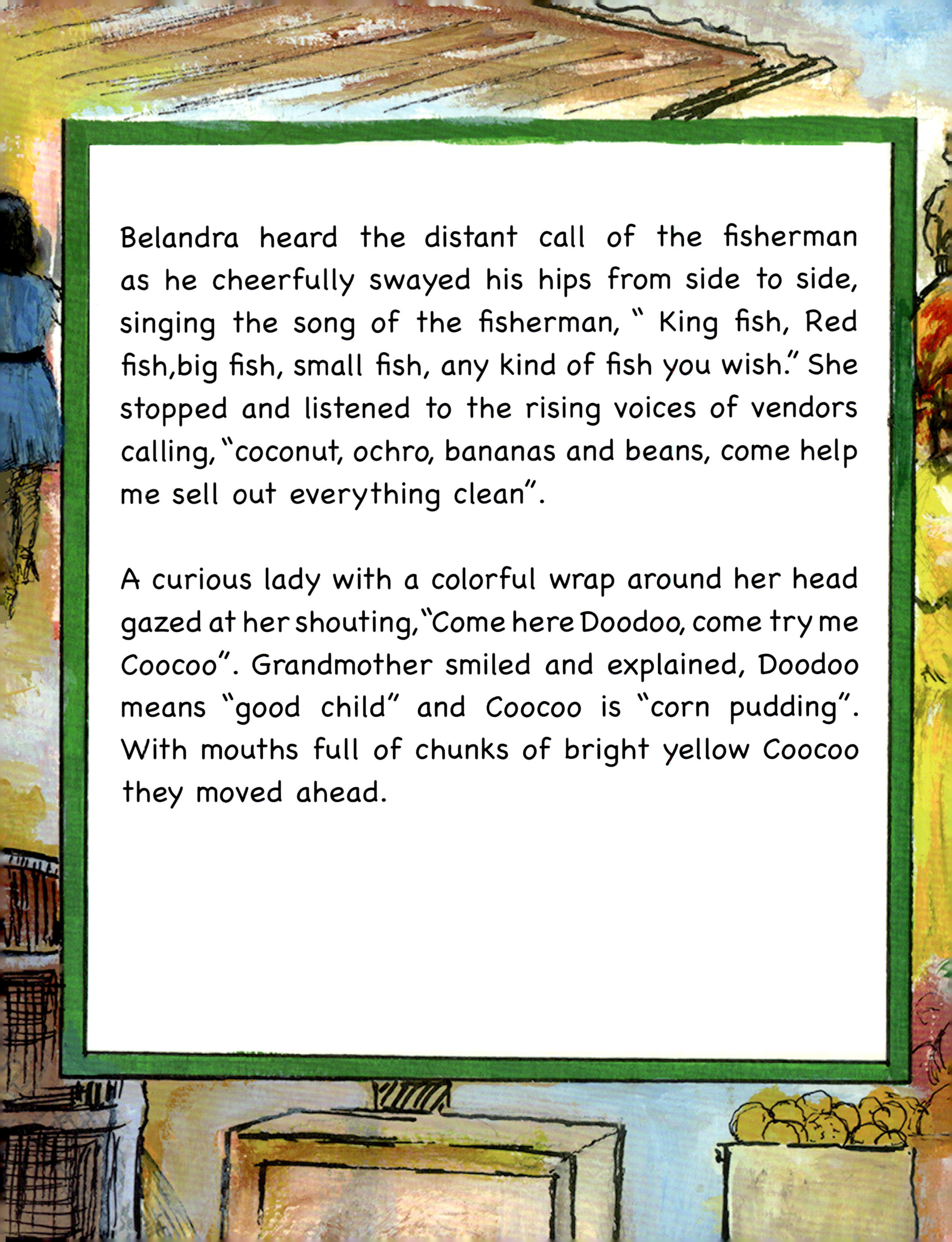

Belandra heard the distant call of the fisherman as he cheerfully swayed his hips from side to side, singing the song of the fisherman, " King fish, Red fish,big fish, small fish, any kind of fish you wish." She stopped and listened to the rising voices of vendors calling, "coconut, ochro, bananas and beans, come help me sell out everything clean".

A curious lady with a colorful wrap around her head gazed at her shouting,"Come here Doodoo, come try me Coocoo". Grandmother smiled and explained, Doodoo means "good child" and Coocoo is "corn pudding". With mouths full of chunks of bright yellow Coocoo they moved ahead.

Grandmother chatted from vendor to vendor. She must buy at least one item from each of her market friends. She always says, " It makes them happy."

Grandmother even carried treats for almost every vendor she knew.

In her brown basket there was candy for the fruit vendor, sweet cakes for the vegetable vendor and sugar buns for the egg man. She always says, "It makes them happy".

Our baskets were now full of potatoes, tomatoes, eddoes and cassava, pineapple, papaya, plums and banana. Of course we could not forget about treats for Lolla and Lossa.

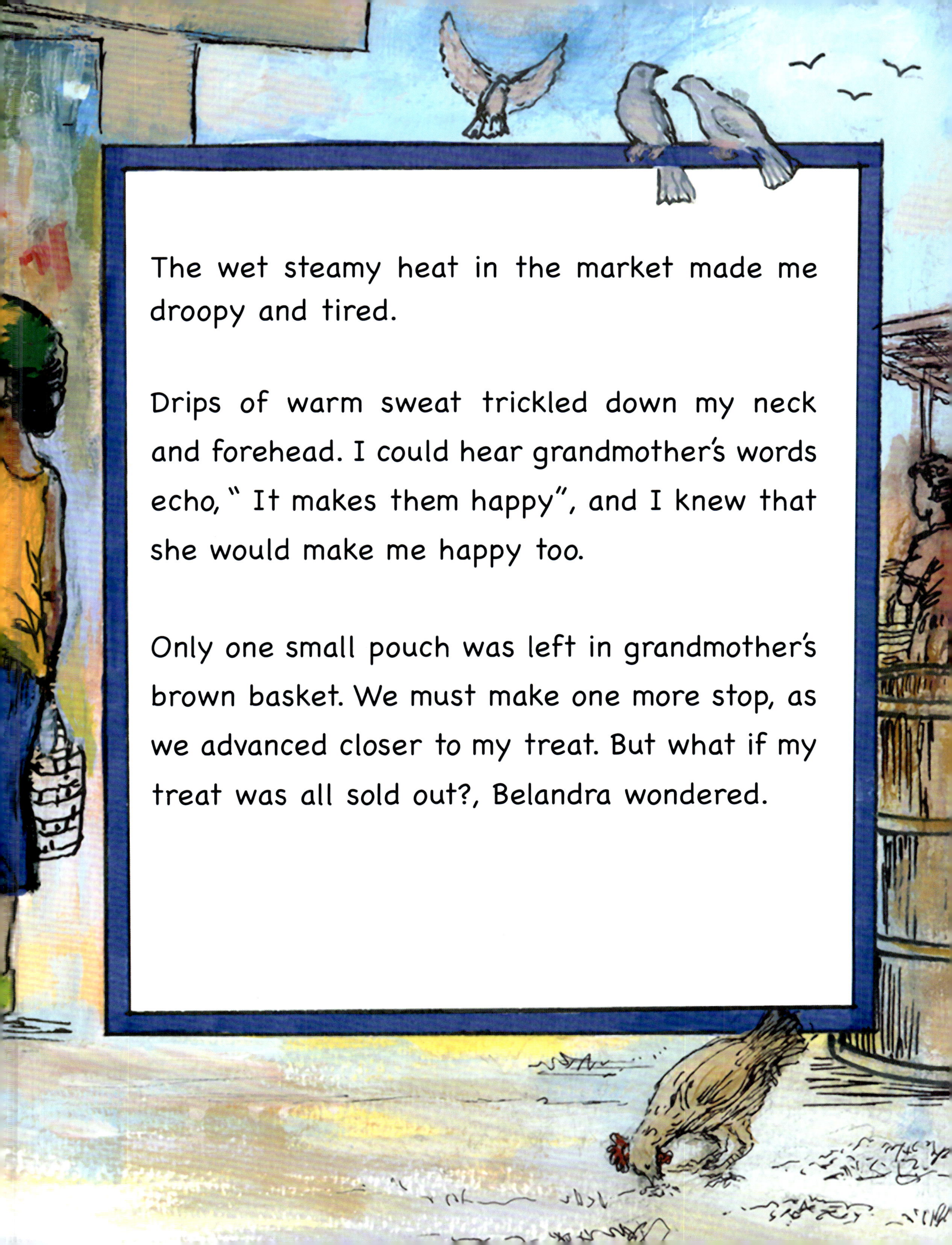

The wet steamy heat in the market made me droopy and tired.

Drips of warm sweat trickled down my neck and forehead. I could hear grandmother's words echo, " It makes them happy", and I knew that she would make me happy too.

Only one small pouch was left in grandmother's brown basket. We must make one more stop, as we advanced closer to my treat. But what if my treat was all sold out?, Belandra wondered.

I stretched my neck out and stared with fear into the corner stall, hoping to glimpse fruits of green, yellow and red colors rising in heaps. My eyes darted all around.

All I saw were empty boxes, crates and baskets. My mouth fell wide open.

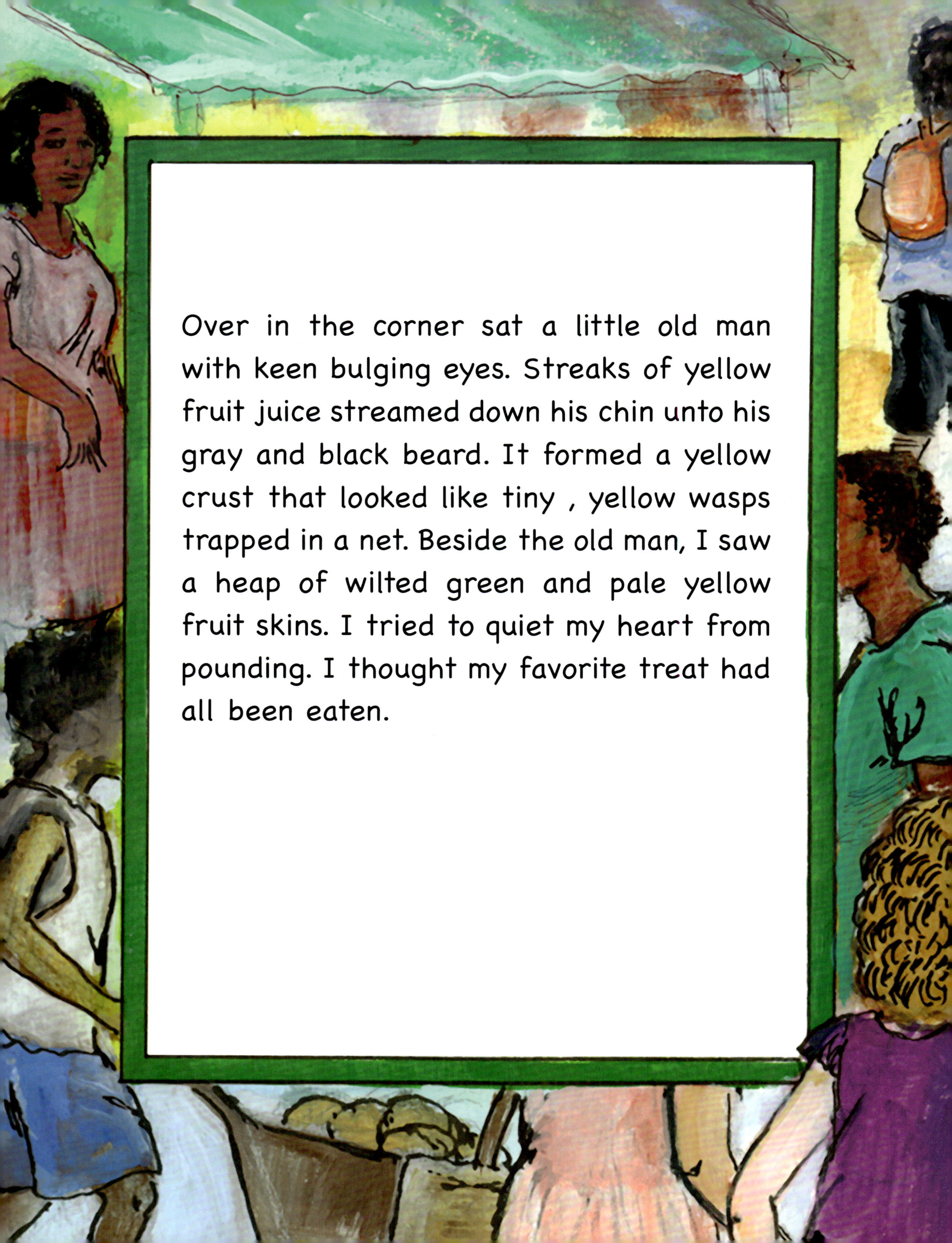

Over in the corner sat a little old man with keen bulging eyes. Streaks of yellow fruit juice streamed down his chin unto his gray and black beard. It formed a yellow crust that looked like tiny , yellow wasps trapped in a net. Beside the old man, I saw a heap of wilted green and pale yellow fruit skins. I tried to quiet my heart from pounding. I thought my favorite treat had all been eaten.

Grandmother said, "Hi Mr. Marty, meet my cute Belandra."

Mr. Marty greeted us with a broad grin. His jaws expanded and exposed his toothless shining gums. Mr. Marty smiled and winked at me. He crouched to reach under a small wooden table. Grandmother had asked Mr. Marty to save me my favorite treat,

A basket-full of mangoes!

GUAVA
JAM

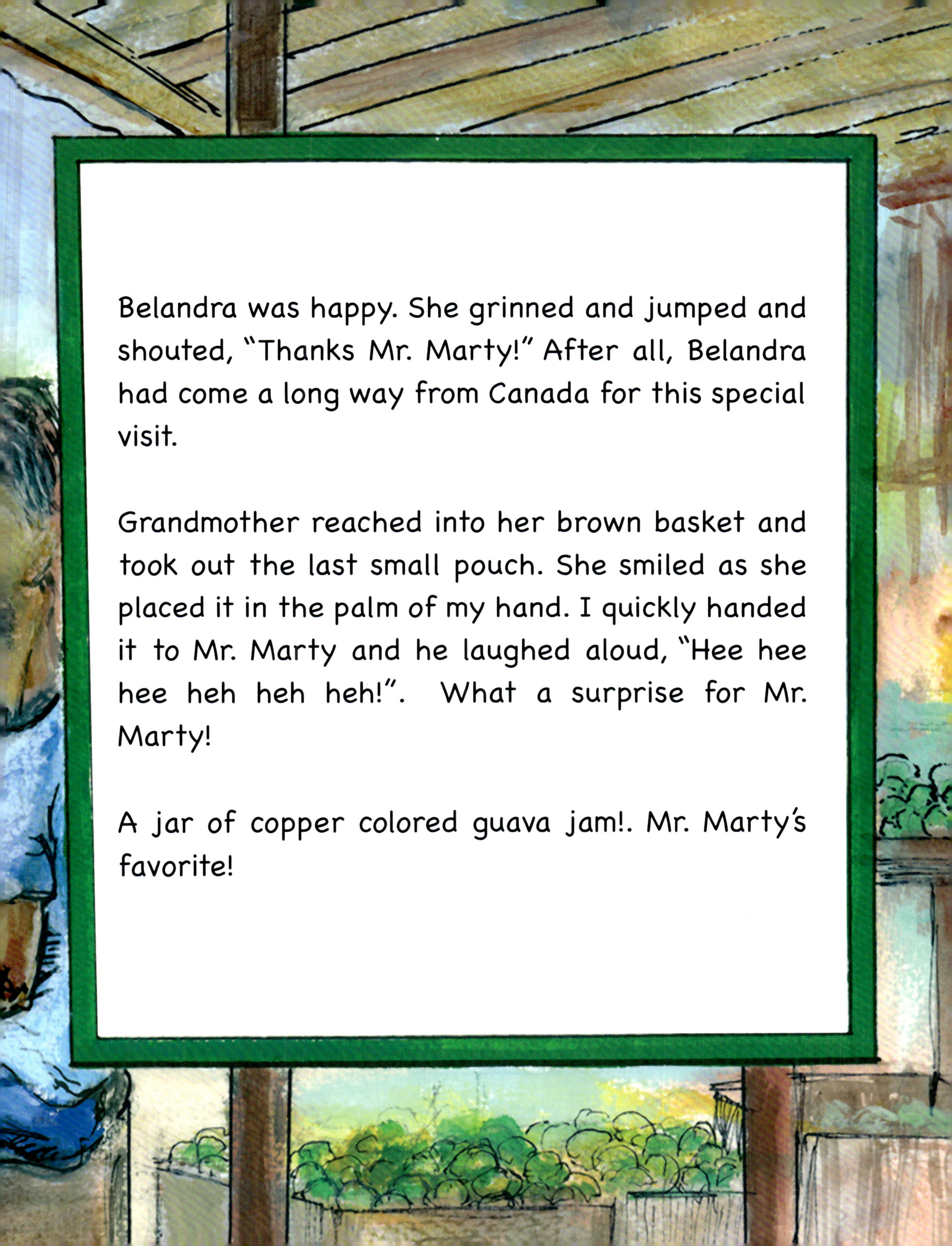

Belandra was happy. She grinned and jumped and shouted, "Thanks Mr. Marty!" After all, Belandra had come a long way from Canada for this special visit.

Grandmother reached into her brown basket and took out the last small pouch. She smiled as she placed it in the palm of my hand. I quickly handed it to Mr. Marty and he laughed aloud, "Hee hee hee heh heh heh!". What a surprise for Mr. Marty!

A jar of copper colored guava jam!. Mr. Marty's favorite!

We hurried home after a busy and fun-filled morning. Lolla and Lossa with tails wagging, anxiously greeted us on the front porch.

They gobbled up their treats of munchie, crunchy meat chews and huge milky biscuits.

Later in the day, Belandra remembered the crumbs she had saved from the breakfast table. As the sun began to set Belandra fed the chicks and made them happy too.

As night time drew closer, Belandra exclaimed, "Oh how I wish and wish for many more fun days with grandmother. To be with grandmother is truly a special treat!"